PAUL'S PLACE

by Judy Driscoll

First published by AuthorHouse 08/09/04

ISBN: 1-4184-5224-6 (sc)

Printed in the United States of America
Bloomington, Indiana

This book is printed on acid-free paper.

authorHOUSE
Your Voice in Print

1663 LIBERTY DRIVE
BLOOMINGTON, INDIANA 47403
(800) 839-8640
www.authorhouse.com

*Like the body itself, a town grows
and changes. Stores change names,
are remodeled, or even replaced, but
the skeleton of yesterday remains,
shaping the dreams of tomorrow.
It is to the builders of these aged
foundations, with their eyes on the future,
the pioneers of Poulsbo, that this book
is dedicated.* – JD

Natives visited in canoe,
Cougars, bears, and deer came to
this land where trees so thickly grew,

"Oh, oh, do you see that bear? We've been gathering clams to take home to Old Man House where our people, the Suquamish, live. We come here often to hunt ducks or gather shellfish. We also catch many dogfish in this bay. Dried dogfish skin makes a good scraper for smoothing our canoes. I hope Brother Bear leaves quickly without eating all our clams!"

but no one lived at Paul's Place.

There is no record of Native Americans living on Dogfish Bay, but they did come here to hunt and fish.

Another name for a dogfish is a sand shark. The skin of a dogfish is very rough. When it is dried, it can be used in the same way we use sandpaper today.

Explorers sailed in white-winged boats.
Surveyors mapped with many notes
naming coves and points and coasts,

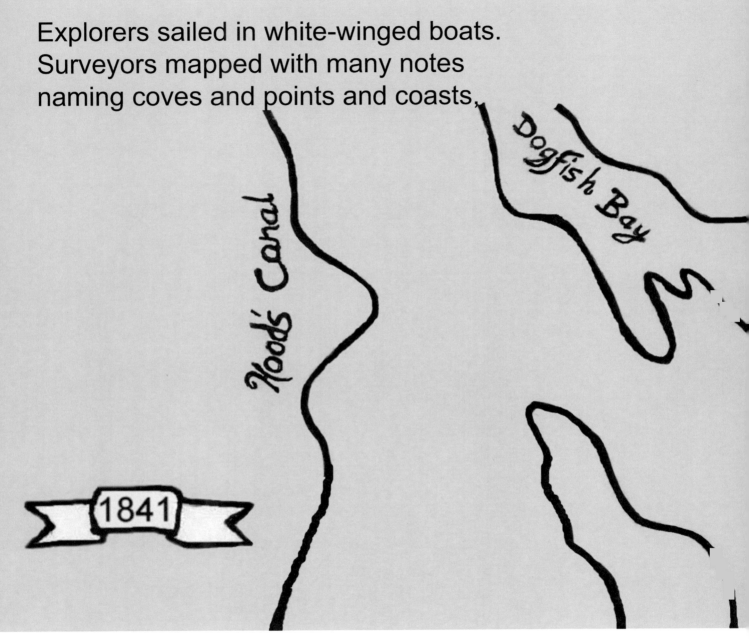

Dogfish Bay

Hood's Canal

1841

In 1792 Capt. George Vancouver in his sloop DISCOVERY came into Puget Sound. With his men he began charting and surveying the land for the Hudson's Bay Company. He named Mt. Rainier, Mt. Baker, Whidbey Island, Point Defiance, Puget Sound, and Hood's Canal, among other places we know.

The Suquamish called Vancouver's ship "a house with white wings that goes on the water."

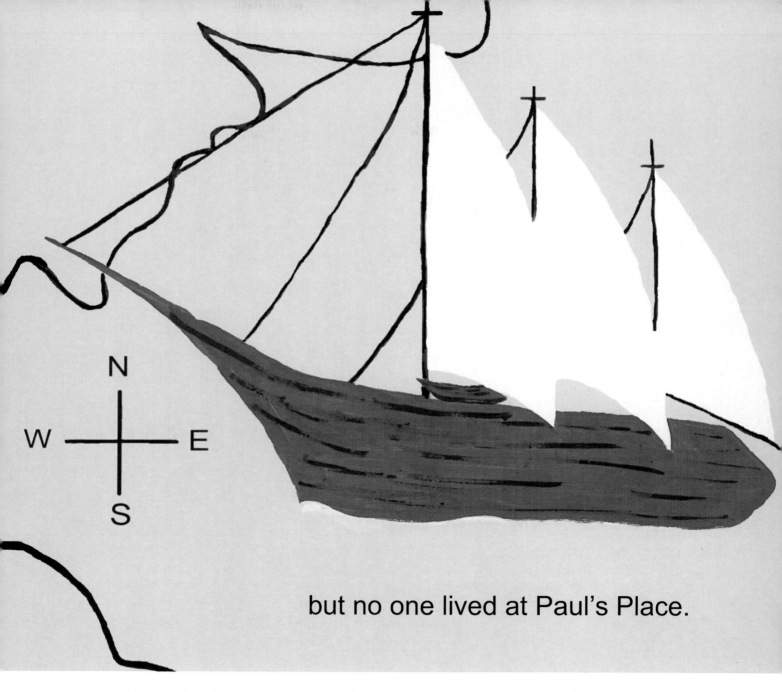

but no one lived at Paul's Place.

It wasn't until 1841 that Americans, under Lt. Charles Wilkes, surveyed Puget Sound. His men named places we visit often like Agate Passage and Bainbridge Island.

Loggers came and felled the best
firs and cedars without rest,
leaving stump and broken nest,

T-i-i-i-m-m-m-b-e-r-r-r-! Firs and cedars grew so close together on Dogfish Bay that loggers couldn't use horses or oxen to help them. They cut down the trees closest to the shore and felled them into the bay. The floating logs were corralled into a loop of chained logs. This *log boom* was towed behind a tugboat to the lumber mill at Port Madison on Bainbridge Island.

but no one lived at Paul's Place.

When felling gigantic cedars, loggers cut notches in the tree trunk to hold springboards. Two men with a long saw stood on the springboards and cut high on the tree trunk where the wood grain was straight. Some of these old, notched, tree trunks can still be seen along our roads.

Then came Paul Wahl with ox and crew,
Eley, Prescott, and Hurdleboo,
building skids and bridges, too,

Soon the trees closest to the shore were gone. Loggers like Paul Wahl and Stener Thorsen brought in oxen and built trestle bridges and corduroy roads back a mile from the shore. Paul Wahl's first landing was at the foot of Jensen Way in downtown Poulsbo. There he built a cook shack and a bunk house.

but no one lived at Paul's Place.

A corduroy road was made by splitting small logs in half and laying them across the trail. The logs were then greased. Now logs wouldn't bog down in the mud. It would have been a bumpy ride for us, but a great skid for logs! Hostmark Street and Jensen Way were used as early skid roads.

1883

Eliason and Olson came,
buying land, the wild to tame.
Eliason stayed, but still no name

"Oh my aching arms!" Jorgen Eliason and Peter Olson rowed a boat across Puget Sound from Seattle to visit their friend Ole Stubb. Ole lived near what is now Keyport on Dogfish Bay. They liked the land across the bay and decided to take out homesteads on it. Peter Olson soon sold his land. Jorgen Eliason decided to stay and make his home here. He lived in the old cook shack until his house was built.

was given the land called Paul's Place.

When it was ready, Jorgen Eliason brought his eight-year-old son, E.J., and his sister, Rachel, from Seattle to their new home. Their house was near the present day Hostmark Apartments. Mr. Eliason donated a corner of his land for the first church in town, Fordefjord Menighed, (now First Lutheran Church) and the cemetery behind it.

I.B. Moe, with all his sons,
moved to the bay and logged by tons.
He ordered mail. Now a steamer comes

Iver Moe moved to Dogfish Bay just one month after Jorgen Eliason. He brought his wife and three sons, Albert, Andrew, and Chris. Andrew Moe was Poulsbo's first mayor. Albert Moe was a logger and farmer. Chris Moe was a steamer captain in the Mosquito Fleet.

The many small steamers that scurried about Puget Sound were nicknamed the Mosquito Fleet.

once a week to Paul's Place.

The steamer AUGUSTA came once a week bringing supplies and mail to a float in the bay. Someone would row out to the float and bring in whatever the steamer left.

The town was named by Mr. Moe.
His cursive 'a' looked like an 'o.'
Paul's Place in Norwegian is spelled
"P<u>a</u>ulsbo,"
but the postmaster spelled it
"P<u>o</u>ulsbo."

1886

Paulsbo was the name of Mr. Moe's hometown in Norway. That may be why he chose the name. However, some people think he named our town in honor of Paul Wahl's landing. Maybe it was both!

Post Office Department,

OFFICE OF THE FIRST ASSISTANT P. M. GENERAL,

WASHINGTON, D. C., _Sept 9_, 188 6

Sir: Before the Postmaster General decides upon the application for the establishment of a post office at _Poulsbo_, County of _Kitsap_, State of _Washington_, it is necessary for you to carefully answer the subjoined questions, get a neighboring postmaster to certify ... and return the location paper to the Department, addressed to me. If the site selected ... be supplied with ... point on the nearest mail route by a "Special Office" can be established ... a sum equal to two-thirds of ... of the postmaster at such office with ... carrier, for ...

... contractor, or person performing service for ... and require him to execute the ... certificate as to the practicability of supplying the proposed ... and return the same to the Department.

Very respectfully,

A. E. Stevenson

First Assistant Postmaster General.

To Mr. _C. B. W. Made_

care of the Postmaster of _____, who will please forward to him.

STATEMENT

The proposed office to be called _Poulsbo_

☞ Select a name for the proposed office, which, when written, will not resemble name of any other post office in the State.

It will be situated in the S ¼ of Section _Ten_, Township _26_ (North or South) _North_, Range _One_ (East or West), in the County of _Kitsap_, State of _Washington_ ...

to _Port Townsend_ ... near route No. ... returns per week.

The contractor's name is ...

Will it be directly on this route?—Ans. _No_

If not, how far from, and on which side of it?—Ans. _about 11 m ... called route & West_

How much will it INCREASE the travel of the mail one way each trip?—Ans. ...

Where will the mail leave the present route to supply the proposed office?—Ans. _Port ... Wash-_

What post office will be left out by this change?—Ans. _none_

If not on any route, is a "Special Office"... _Yes_ To be supplied from _Port ...._

The name of the nearest office on the same route ... is _Port Madison_

Its distance is _(?) ... water_ ... direction from ...

The name of the nearest office to the proposed one, not on this route, is _Port Gamble_ ... direction from the ...

Its distance is _by ... g ... y. by water_ ... about eleven miles ... ... direction from the proposed office.

The name of the most direct ... prominent river near it is ...

The name of the nearest creek is _Poulsbo Creek_

The proposed office will be ... on the ...

... it, and will be _two feet_ ... miles from ... creek, on the _West_ ... side of it

If on the line of ... railroad is _North West_ ...

... railroad, on which side will ... how far from the track; and what is, or will be, the name of the station? ... ...

What will be the distance from ... station?—Ans. _40 miles_

State name of station ...

What will be the distance from the proposed ... which mail trains make regular stops?—Ans. _40_

State name of station? _in file_

If the proposed office is located ...

... express charge, with the name to be carried or sent from the proposed ... expense on the Department ...

If it is a village, state the number of inhabitants.—Ans. ...

Also, the population to be supplied by the proposed office.—Ans. ...

A diagram, on this form a map, showing the position of the proposed ... neighboring river or creek, roads, and other ...

... or will be agreed upon, will be needed and is therefore desired.

A correct map of the locality to be furnished by the county surveyor, ... without expense to the Post office ...

... I certify ... to be correct and true, according to the best of my knowledge and belief, this _24th_ day of _September_, 188 6.

(☞ Sign full name.)

_C. B. W. ..._

I CERTIFY that I have examined the foregoing statement, and that it is correct and true ... of my knowledge and belief.

_..._

Postmaster

POULSBO, SEP 24 1886 WASH.

Look at the spelling of Poulsbo in the magnifying glasses. Do you see why the postmaster got confused and misspelled it? Learn to write neatly and clearly. Someday you, too, might name a town!

The first post office was in Mr. Moe's house. After Mr. Hostmark opened his store in Poulsbo, it was easier for people to get their mail at the store than to go to Moe's house, so the post office was moved to Hostmark's store.

Hostmark's building still stands on the corner of Jensen Way and Front Street. It is the oldest building in town. Look for the historical marker on its front.

Be careful to answer the inquiries fully and accurately, or the case will not be acted upon.

Adolph Hostmark built a store
in an old cook shack quite near the shore.
Christiansen and Langeland bore

There goes E.J. running out of town. He was in Hostmark's store playing with the padlock to the mailbag and accidentally locked it before it was put on the bag. But the key to the lock was not at the store. This would never do! The mailbag must not travel unlocked, and the steamer was coming!

E.J. began running to Mr. Moe's house to get the key. He ran and ran without stopping, more than a mile.

their goods in boats to Poulsbo.

He arrived too out of breath to tell Mrs. Moe what he needed. At last he was able to tell her he needed the key. Mrs. Moe hung it on a chain around his neck, and E.J. started running again...over a mile back to the store!

"Sorry E.J., the steamer left the bay just before you got here! The mailbag went to Seattle unlocked."

In 1898 E.J. Eliason became the postmaster for Poulsbo. He was the postmaster for twenty-seven years!

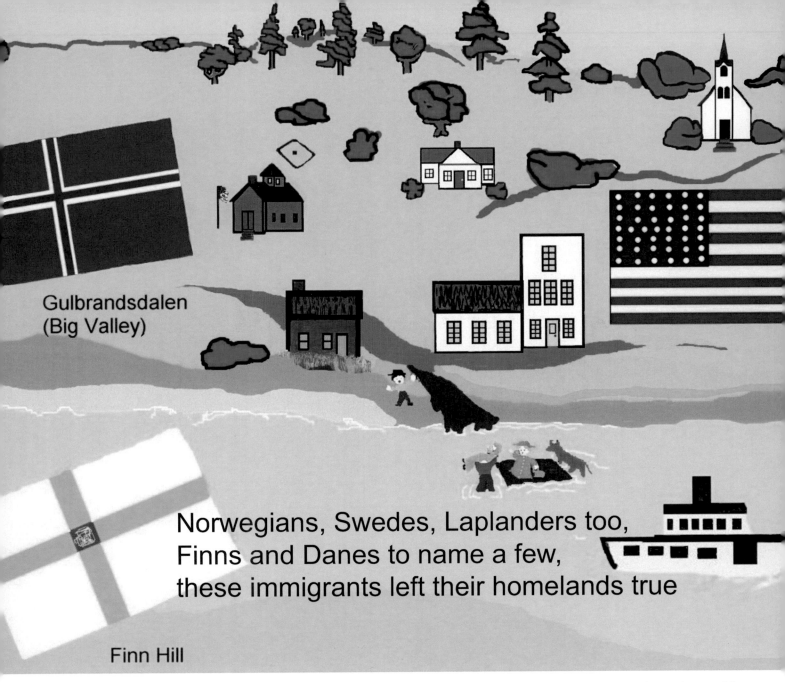

Gulbrandsdalen
(Big Valley)

Finn Hill

Norwegians, Swedes, Laplanders too,
Finns and Danes to name a few,
these immigrants left their homelands true

When the steamer came, cows and horses on board were pushed into the water to swim ashore. Young Alfred Hostmark earned a few cents by carrying the ladies to shore from the float to keep their shoes and long dresses dry. There he is right now with a lovely lady in his arms.

Lemolo

1889

Scandia

to start new lives in Poulsbo.

"What are you doing, E.J.? Oh, I see." Jorgen's cow wandered away. An older boy and E.J. were sent to find her. They searched along the shoreline to Suquamish where they found Old Bessie. On the way home, the tide was high. The creek they had crossed easily before was now too deep for E.J. who couldn't swim. He grabbed the last thing he saw as the cow crossed ahead of him -- the cow's tail! There he is bobbing and spinning like a trolling spoon on a fishing line! "Hang on, E.J.!"

Over the years, the village grew
as folks built schools and churches new.
Poultry farms and fishing crews

When the biggest trees were gone, the settlers turned to farming and fishing to earn a living. The Pacific Coast Cod Fish Co. was built on the waterfront south of town. Many people worked there packing fish when the fishing boats came in from Alaska. Boat building was also a big business.

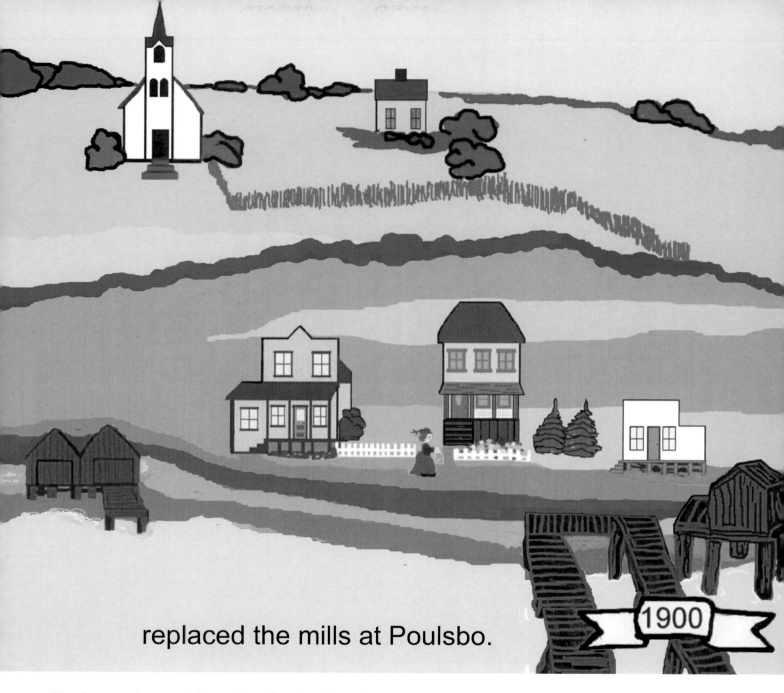

replaced the mills at Poulsbo.

1900

The farmers began dairy and poultry farming. Some of them raised fruit. Their wives would churn butter and gather eggs. Then once a week the wives would take their butter, eggs, and fruit aboard a steamer and travel to Seattle to sell them at the Seattle Public Market.

Late in May the folks all came
to the Children's Home,
Martha - Mary its name,

GRANDVIEW HOTEL

1910

Martha and Mary Children's Home cared for homeless children. Some of them were orphans. Many of them were children without mothers whose fathers were fishing in Alaska. The home was a large farm in Poulsbo, stretching from today's Martha and Mary Care Center to the back of Poulsbo Place. Ebenezer Home, still a home for seniors on the hill, was part of the same farm.

for picnic treats and lots of games -
Decoration Day in Poulsbo.

The Children's Home received day old bread from the Star Bakery. Children helped tend the vegetable and fruit gardens. The older boys milked the cows. Everyone helped churn the butter.

Decoration Day was the forerunner of Poulsbo's Viking Fest. Sometimes as many as 7,000 people from around Puget Sound arrived on steamers and spent the day visiting with the children at Martha and Mary.

In the middle of the night,
Mrs. Myreboe had a fright!
"Fire! Fire!"
Flames leaping bright

Fred Frederickson was asleep in the Olympic Hotel Annex when he heard screams. He saw flames in the hallway and jumped out his window. Then he ran to get one of the new round-bottomed fire buckets. The buckets had never been used and were stored in a locked shed.

attacked the heart of Poulsbo!

The men quickly formed a bucket brigade. Hand over hand the buckets traveled from the bay to the fire. Fighting the fire one bucket at a time took all night. The steamers HYAK and ATHLON helped by connecting their pumps together and spraying water on the buildings near the bay.

In the morning, without a sound,
rising smoke hung black and brown.
Eight stores in ashes on the ground.

When the fireboat from Seattle arrived in the morning, it was too late. The fire was already out. Eight businesses had burned to the ground. They were the Olympic Hotel, a hardware store, Twedt's Barber Shop, a millinery shop, a tailor shop, Paulson - Hostmark - Borgen Furniture Store, Brevig's Star Bakery, and Young's garage.

The sky was gray in Poulsbo.

Years later, Aleda Seierstad, who was a young girl at the time of the fire, recalled walking down Front St. on her way to school the morning after the fire. She found pieces of brightly colored, stained glass melted on the dirt road in front of the destroyed hotel. She kept them as remembrances of her shock at the devastation of the fire.

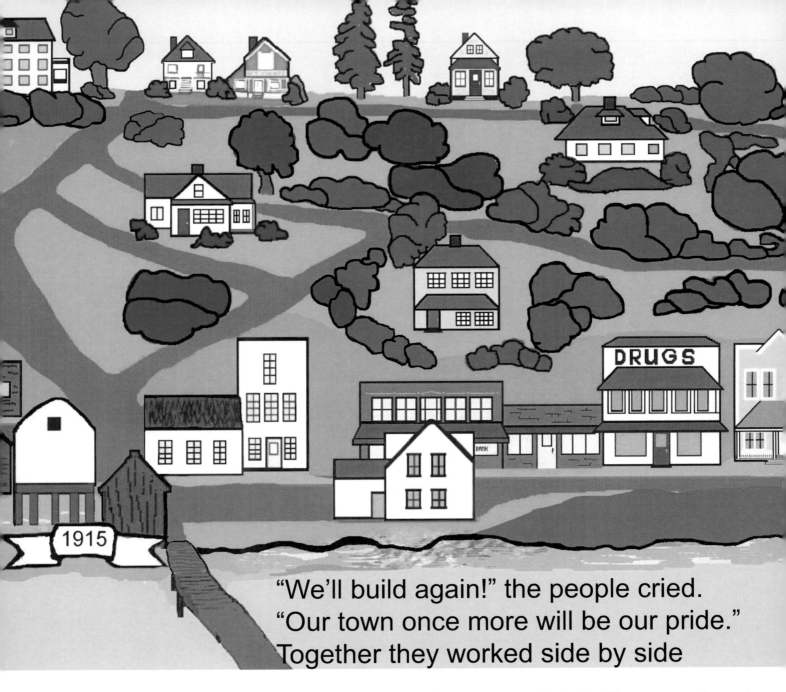

1915

"We'll build again!" the people cried.
"Our town once more will be our pride."
Together they worked side by side

In early Poulsbo, the water came nearly to the edge of the street during high tide. The stores on the water side of Front St. were built on piers. When the piers caught fire, the stores burned very quickly. After the fire, most of the stores were built out of brick and cement. Today the Olympic Hotel, Young's Block, and the Myreboe building still stand. All of them were built in 1915.

rebuilding the town of Poulsbo.

Another brick building in the center of the block near Hostmark's store was also built in 1915. It was once a bank. Look for the old bank vault in the back of one of the shops.

One hundred years on the bay so blue,
the old still stands beside the new.

During the 1950's, part of the waterfront was filled in with boulders. This allowed the stores to sit on rocks instead of piers and also made space for a parking lot behind the stores.

A logging camp that grew. . .

In order to connect two parking lots, one long building, Rindal & Ness Feed Store, was cut in two. Today cars are driven between the two buildings that used to be one.

and grew. . .

In the 1970's, the waterfront was again filled in to provide the waterfront park, a new marina and Kvelstad Pavilion.

The large boulder in the park was pulled out of the bottom of Liberty Bay when the park was being built. Scientists call it an *erratic*, which means it is a rock out of place. It was carried to Poulsbo from the far north by a glacier during the ice age.

into the town of Poulsbo.

From the ice age to the space age, Poulsbo is, indeed, both old and new.

The End . . .
or maybe just the beginning!

About the Author

When Judy Driscoll moved to Poulsbo, she was enchanted with the beauty of the village on the bay and intrigued with the history and tales of its early pioneers. <u>Paul's Place</u> is the product of her love of sharing that history with her students. Because her annual walking tour of historic Poulsbo was so well received by both students and their parents, it seemed only natural to compile her research into this stroll through local history. This is her first book.